MASTERING SOCIAL MEDIA

A Comprehensive Guide to Boosting Your Business and Avoiding Pitfalls

Contents

Introduction 4

    The Power of Social Media for Business 7

Utilizing Virtual Entertainment Stages for Brand Mindfulness...12

    Developing Significant areas of fortitude for a Presence 15

    Partner with Your Vested party 18

Case Studies: Successful Businesses and Their Social Media Strategies 22

Social Media Analytics and Measurement.....29

    Grasping Measurements: What to Track and Why..29

    Devices for Observing and Investigating Virtual Entertainment Execution 32

    Deciphering Information to Refine Your Technique 34

Likely Traps: How Online Entertainment Can Damage Your Business 38

    Negative Receptiveness and Notoriety Shrewdness..38

    Controlling Savages and Negative Remarks .40

    Guaranteed and Moral Thoughts 41

    Structures for Easing off: 42

Protecting Your Business on Social Media 46

    Carrying out Online Entertainment Arrangements and Rules 46

    Keeping up with Straightforwardness and Credibility 49

Future Trends in Social Media and Business .. 52

    Arising Stages and Advancements 52

    The Development of Social Business 54

    Expectations for the Future Scene of Online Entertainment 56

Conclusion 59

    Synopsis of Central issues: 59

Introduction

In the present computerized age, the effect of web-based entertainment on organizations couldn't possibly be more significant. Online entertainment stages have changed the manner in which organizations cooperate with their clients, market their items or administrations, and assemble their brands. Whether you're a little neighborhood business or a worldwide partnership, having areas of strength for a via web-based entertainment has become basic for progress in the cutting edge commercial center.

This guide investigates the diverse connection between web-based entertainment and business, digging into how these stages can either move your organization higher than ever or present critical difficulties on the off chance that not oversaw really. We'll look at the different manners by which online entertainment can help your business, from expanding brand attention to encouraging significant associations with your interest group. Furthermore, we'll examine the potential traps that organizations might experience via online entertainment and give procedures to alleviating chances and safeguarding your image's standing.

Through contextual analyses, down to earth tips, and experiences into arising patterns, this guide means to outfit you with the information and devices important to saddle the force of online entertainment for business development. Whether you're a carefully prepared advertiser or simply beginning, understanding the subtleties of online entertainment can have a significant effect in accomplishing your business goals in the present serious scene.

Thus, we should make a plunge and investigate how virtual entertainment can be a unique advantage for your business.

The Power of Social Media for Business

Web-based entertainment has altered the manner in which organizations convey, market, and associate with their crowd. Here is a more critical glance at how web-based entertainment can be a strong instrument for business development:

Brand Mindfulness: Virtual entertainment stages furnish organizations with a worldwide stage to exhibit their image character, values, and contributions. Through connecting with content and designated informing, organizations can contact a huge crowd and secure themselves as industry pioneers.

Client Commitment: Web-based entertainment considers direct connection with clients continuously. Whether through remarks, messages, or live visits, organizations can draw in with their crowd, address concerns, and give customized help, encouraging more grounded connections and client devotion.

Statistical surveying: Web-based entertainment stages offer important experiences into purchaser inclinations, ways of behaving, and drifts. By checking discussions, investigating commitment measurements, and directing reviews, organizations can accumulate noteworthy information to illuminate item advancement, advertising systems, and business choices.

Driving Site Traffic: Web-based entertainment fills in as a strong driver of site traffic. By sharing convincing substance and advancements, organizations can tempt devotees to visit their site, investigate items or administrations, and at last make buys.

Lead Age: Web-based entertainment stages give chances to lead age through designated promoting, supported content, and vital associations. By arriving at potential clients where they invest their energy on the web, organizations can draw in qualified leads and support them through the deals channel.

Brand Backing: Fulfilled clients frequently become brand advocates via online entertainment, imparting their positive encounters to companions and adherents. Utilizing client produced content and empowering client tributes can intensify brand promotion, prompting expanded believability and verbal exchange references.

Upper hand: Keeping a functioning presence via web-based entertainment can furnish organizations with an upper hand. By keeping up to date with industry patterns, checking contenders' exercises, and adjusting systems likewise, organizations can situate themselves as creative and responsive forerunners in their field.

Financially savvy Showcasing: Contrasted with customary promoting channels, web-based entertainment advertising is many times more practical and quantifiable. With choices for both natural and paid advancement, organizations, everything being equal, can use online entertainment to arrive at their interest group without burning through every last dollar.

Generally, virtual entertainment offers organizations unmatched open doors for development, brand building, and client commitment. By outfitting the force of these stages in a calculated manner, organizations can open new roads for outcome in the present powerful computerized scene.

Utilizing Virtual Entertainment Stages for Brand Mindfulness

Virtual diversion stages go about areas of strength for as for growing brand care and reaching a greater group. This is the manner in which associations can truly utilize these stages to assist with marking detectable quality:

Pick the Right Stages: Perceive the virtual amusement stages where your vested party is by and large powerful. Whether it's Facebook, Instagram, Twitter, LinkedIn, or others, revolve your undertakings around the stages that line up with your goal portion and business targets.

Upgrade Your Profiles: Make persuading and consistent profiles across all web-based diversion stages. Use extraordinary pictures, associating with portrayals, and appropriate watchwords to convey your picture character and attract aficionados.

Share Attracting Fulfilled: Reliably share grouped and interfacing with content that resounds with your group. This can consolidate blog passages, accounts, infographics, overviews, and client created content. Keep your substance new, appropriate, and agreed with your picture values to enchant your group's thought.

Use Visuals: Visual substance will overall perform better by means of online diversion, so merge eye-getting pictures, accounts, and plans into your posts. Visuals grab thought as well as help with passing on your picture message, as a matter of fact.

Support Sharing and Responsibility: Develop responsibility with your group by engaging preferences, comments, offers, and names. Look for explanation on major problems, run difficulties, and brief followers to share their experiences to extend your compass and heighten your picture message.

Collaborate with Forces to be reckoned with: Teaming up with forces to be reckoned with or industry experts can help with introducing your picture to a greater group and build legitimacy. Recognize forces to be reckoned with who line up with your picture values and vested party, and work together on fulfilled creation or upheld posts.

Developing Significant areas of fortitude for a Presence

A strong online presence is basic for associations wanting to hang out in the mechanized scene. Here are key procedures for building and keeping areas of strength for a based presence:

Make a Specialist Site: Your site fills in as the modernized retail exterior for your business. Promise it is ostensibly captivating, simple to utilize, and upgraded for web files. Give huge substance, clear course, and normal intend to further develop the client experience.

Advance for Web search apparatuses: Execute site smoothing out (Web improvement) best practices to deal with your website's detectable quality in web crawler results. Lead expression research, upgrade meta marks, and make quality substance to attract normal busy time gridlock to your site.

Unsurprising Stamping: Stay aware of consistent checking across each and every web based channel, including your webpage, virtual diversion profiles, email handouts, and electronic takes note. Use unsurprising assortments, text based styles, logos, and illuminating to develop your picture character and empower memorability.

Attract with Your Group: Successfully attract with your group across various online stages. Answer comments, messages, and studies in an ideal and master way. Show appreciation for positive analysis and address any concerns or demands quickly.

Share Significant Substance: Regularly convey huge and appropriate substance that educates, draws in, or rouses your principal vested party. This can integrate blog sections, articles, context oriented examinations, accounts, computerized broadcasts, and that is just a hint of something larger. Give deals with any consequences regarding your group's pain points and secure yourself as a trusted in master in your industry.

Screen Web based Standing: Screen notification of your picture on the web and proactively manage your web based standing. Address any terrible information or overviews skillfully and hope to decide issues to keep a positive brand picture.

Partner with Your Vested party

Strong correspondence and relationship with your vested party are essential for building huge associations and driving business advancement. This is the manner in which associations can connect with their fundamental vested party through web-based diversion:

Handle Your Group: Cut out a valuable open door to fathom your vested party's economics, interests, tendencies, and trouble spots. Use virtual diversion examination and client encounters to moreover obtain significant pieces of information into their approach to acting and designer your illuminating.

Make Buyer Personas: Cultivate point by point buyer personas that address your ideal clients. This will help you with putting forth assigned content and publicizing attempts that reverberate with express pieces of your group.

Modify Your Illuminating: Personalization is basic to connecting with your group on a more significant level. Tailor your illuminating and content to address the excellent necessities and interests of different group segments. Use language, tone, and imagery that reverberates with your principal vested party.

Partake in Conversations: Actually take part in conversations with your group by means of electronic diversion. Answer comments, messages, and notification right away and truly. Show authentic interest in your group's requests, analysis, and experiences.

Offer some motivation: Focus on offering an advantage to your group through your electronic diversion content. Offer important hints, encounters, and resources that address their hardships and help them with achieving their targets. Position your picture as a trusted in resource and associate in their journey.

Be Veritable: Validness is critical for building trust and authenticity with your group. Be genuine, clear, and genuine in your coordinated efforts and correspondences. Share behind the scenes content, stories, and experiences that refine your picture and resonate with your group on a singular level.

By using virtual diversion arranges truly, associations can further develop brand care, create significant solid areas for a presence, and production critical relationship with their ideal vested party, finally driving business result in the electronic age.

Case Studies: Successful Businesses and Their Social Media Strategies

Breaking down genuine instances of organizations that have utilized virtual entertainment actually can give important experiences and motivation to your own online entertainment system. The following are a couple of contextual investigations of organizations that have flourished through their inventive and key utilization of online entertainment:

Nike

Outline: Nike is a worldwide activewear and footwear brand known for its notable swoosh logo and strong promoting efforts. The organization has effectively used virtual entertainment to interface with its crowd and support its image personality.

Web-based Entertainment Methodology: Nike's virtual entertainment system centers around narrating, local area commitment, and client produced content. The brand shares motivating accounts of competitors, advances its items through outwardly dazzling symbolism and recordings, and energizes client support through hashtags like #JustDoIt.

Influence: Nike's drawing in virtual entertainment content has assisted it with building areas of strength for a devoted following across stages like Instagram, Twitter, and Facebook. The brand's missions, for example, the "Fantasy Insane" crusade highlighting Colin Kaepernick, have ignited discussions and produced critical buzz, further setting Nike's situation as an innovator in the games business.

Sephora

Outline: Sephora is a global chain of excellence stores known for its large number of beauty care products, skincare, and scent items. The organization has embraced web-based entertainment as a critical channel for interfacing with excellence devotees and driving deals.

Virtual Entertainment Procedure: Sephora's online entertainment methodology rotates around client created content, powerhouse organizations, and intelligent encounters. The brand urges clients to share their cosmetics looks and item proposals utilizing hashtags like #SephoraHaul and #BeautyInsider. Sephora likewise teams up with magnificence powerhouses and hosts virtual occasions and instructional exercises to draw in its crowd.

Influence: Sephora's essential utilization of web-based entertainment has assisted it with developing a dynamic internet based local area and drive client commitment. By exhibiting genuine clients and powerhouses utilizing its items, Sephora has fabricated trust and validity with its crowd, prompting expanded brand faithfulness and deals.

Airbnb

Outline: Airbnb is a web-based commercial center that associates explorers with remarkable facilities all over the planet. The organization has utilized web-based entertainment to exhibit its assorted scope of postings and rouse travel fans.

Web-based Entertainment Technique: Airbnb's virtual entertainment procedure centers around visual narrating and client produced content. The brand curates dazzling photographs and recordings of its facilities, objections, and encounters on stages like Instagram and Pinterest. Airbnb additionally urges hosts and visitors to share their accounts and encounters utilizing hashtags like #Airbnb and #LiveThere.

Influence: Airbnb's convincing online entertainment content has assisted it with building major areas of strength for a presence and draw in voyagers from around the globe. By featuring the special and valid encounters accessible through its foundation, Airbnb has enlivened longing for novelty or adventure and produced buzz, driving both brand mindfulness and appointments.

These contextual analyses outline how organizations across enterprises can use online entertainment to connect with their crowd, build up their image character, and drive business results. By understanding the systems and strategies utilized by effective brands like Nike, Sephora, and Airbnb, organizations can gather important bits of knowledge to illuminate their own virtual entertainment endeavors and make comparative progress.

Social Media Analytics and Measurement

Grasping Measurements: What to Track and Why

Following and breaking down virtual entertainment measurements is fundamental for assessing the adequacy of your online entertainment endeavors and streamlining your procedure for improved results. Here are a critical measurements to track and why they matter:

Commitment Measurements: Commitment measurements, like preferences, remarks, offers, and snaps, measure how your crowd interfaces with your substance. Following commitment assists you with understanding what resounds with your crowd and can illuminate content creation methodologies.

Reach and Impressions: Arrive at alludes to the complete number of exceptional clients who have seen your substance, while impressions address the all out number of times your substance has been shown. Checking reach and impressions gives experiences into the perceivability and reach of your web-based entertainment posts.

Devotee Development: Adherent development tracks the increment or abatement in your online entertainment following over the long run. Observing supporter development assists you with measuring the viability of your substance technique and crowd procurement endeavors.

Reference Traffic: Reference traffic estimates the quantity of guests to your site that come from virtual entertainment stages. Following reference traffic assists you with understanding how virtual entertainment adds to site traffic and transformations.

Change Measurements: Transformation measurements, like active visitor clicking percentage (CTR), transformation rate, and profit from speculation (return on initial capital investment), measure the adequacy of your virtual entertainment crusades in driving wanted activities, for example, site visits, recruits, or buys.

Devices for Observing and Investigating Virtual Entertainment Execution

Various apparatuses are accessible to help organizations screen and break down their online entertainment execution actually. Here are a few famous devices:

Support: Cushion is a web-based entertainment the board stage that permits you to plan posts, track commitment, and break down execution across different virtual entertainment stages.

Hootsuite: Hootsuite is another virtual entertainment the board instrument that offers highlights for planning posts, observing discussions, and examining web-based entertainment measurements.

Sprout Social: Fledgling Social gives devices to web-based entertainment booking, checking, and examination, permitting organizations to follow commitment, measure execution, and produce reports.

Google Examination: Google Examination is an integral asset for following site traffic and dissecting the viability of web-based entertainment crusades in driving transformations and income.

Facebook Bits of knowledge: Facebook Experiences gives nitty gritty examination on your Facebook Page, remembering information for reach, commitment, and socioeconomics of your crowd.

Deciphering Information to Refine Your Technique

Whenever you've gathered information on your virtual entertainment execution, it's vital to examine the information and use bits of knowledge to refine your web-based entertainment procedure. This is the way to successfully decipher information:

Distinguish Patterns and Examples: Search for patterns and examples in your information to recognize what sorts of content perform best, when your crowd is generally dynamic, and which web-based entertainment stages drive the most commitment.

Analyze Execution Over the long run: Look at your virtual entertainment execution over the long run to recognize changes and patterns. Search for factors that might have affected changes in execution, like new happy configurations, missions, or outer occasions.

Benchmark Against Contenders: Benchmark your virtual entertainment execution against contenders to recognize regions where you succeed and regions for development. Break down contenders' techniques, content, and commitment measurements to acquire experiences and thoughts for your own system.

Explore and Repeat: Use information driven bits of knowledge to illuminate examinations and cycles in your virtual entertainment system. Test various sorts of content, posting times, and informing to see what resounds best with your crowd and drives the most commitment.

Put forth Objectives and KPIs: Use information to set explicit, quantifiable objectives and key execution pointers (KPIs) for your web-based entertainment endeavors. Consistently screen progress towards your objectives and change your procedure depending on the situation to improve execution and accomplish your targets.

By figuring out key measurements, using devices for checking and examination, and deciphering information successfully, organizations can refine their virtual entertainment procedure, enhance execution, and accomplish improved brings about coming to and drawing in their main interest group.

Likely Traps: How Online Entertainment Can Damage Your Business

While online entertainment offers various advantages for affiliations, it similarly presents expected dangers and inconveniences. Coming up next are a couple of typical will know about and strategies for working with them:

Negative Receptiveness and Notoriety Shrewdness

Viral Reaction: In the hour of electronic redirection, negative news or clashes wrapping your image can spread quickly and structure into a full scale emergency. This can hurt your image's standing and separate client trust.

Client Battles and Data: Negative assessment or grumblings from clients through electronic redirection stages can stain your image's extra in the event that not tended to supportively and really.

Brand Cunning: Virtual redirection gives a stage to trickiness and phony word to get out expeditiously. On the off chance that your image becomes related with trick or beguiling data, it can hurt your realness and dependability.

Controlling Savages and Negative Remarks

Savage Assaults: Savages and online harassers could focus in on your image with pernicious or ignitable remarks, expecting to incite a response or harm your standing.

Negative Remarks and Audits: Negative remarks, studies, or alerted of your image through electronic redirection can influence public comprehension and redirect likely clients from drawing in with your business.

Managing Assessment: It's basic to answer negative remarks and appraisal incredibly and astoundingly. Disregarding or destroying negative evaluation can fuel what's going on and harm your image's standing further.

Guaranteed and Moral Thoughts

Security Concerns: Gathering and including client information for allocated progressing and showing tries can raise security concerns and real issues, especially with the execution of information insurance rules like GDPR.

Upheld improvement Encroachment: Online redirection stages work on it for clients to share content, yet this likewise grows the bet of protected development encroachment, as unapproved use of brand names, monitored material, or brand resources.

Consistence Dangers: Affiliations should guarantee consistence with fundamental unendingly regulates while driving appearance rehearses through internet based entertainment, including moving principles, purchaser affirmation rules, and industry-unequivocal standards.

Structures for Easing off:

Encourage an Emergency The pioneers Plan: Set up an emergency the board mean to address potential virtual redirection emergencies, as a matter of fact. See key embellishments, spread out correspondence shows, and encourage reaction frameworks for various conditions.

Screen Alerted and Feeling: Utilize online redirection seeing contraptions to follow notice of your image and screen assessment around your things or affiliations. Early area of miserable tendency awards you to pick issues proactively before they raise.

Answer Immediately and Obviously: Answer negative remarks and data quickly and obviously. See concerns, offer approaches or verbalizations of disappointment where fitting, and show an insistence to settling issues.

Instruct Workers: Give arranging and rules to delegates on watchful electronic redirection use and brand portrayal. Request that specialists stay aware of brand respects and remain mindful of stunning limit while associate through virtual redirection, both really and capability.

Look for Valid Appeal: Talk with genuine experts to guarantee consistence with authentic perpetually administers regulating on the web redirection progressing and publicizing. Remain informed about updates to security rules, information assurance makes due, and upheld progress approvals.

By being proactive and executing strategies to address expected gets, affiliations can confine the risks related with online redirection and defend their image notoriety while including the advantages of these stages for progress and responsibility.

Protecting Your Business on Social Media

Carrying out Online Entertainment Arrangements and Rules

Lay out Clear Approaches: Foster complete virtual entertainment strategies and rules that frame adequate use, content principles, protection contemplations, and worker obligations while addressing the organization via web-based entertainment stages.

Teach Workers: Give preparing and instruction to workers via online entertainment arrangements and best practices. Guarantee they grasp their jobs and obligations, including how to deal with delicate data, cooperate with clients, and address the brand expertly.

Screen Consistency: Routinely screen virtual entertainment movement to guarantee consistence with organization strategies and rules. Utilize virtual entertainment checking devices to follow representative connections and recognize any infringement or expected gambles.

Emergency The executives: Taking care of Web-based Entertainment Backfire

Set up an Emergency Reaction Plan: Foster a thorough emergency reaction plan that frames jobs and obligations, correspondence conventions, and heightening techniques in case of a virtual entertainment emergency. Appoint explicit people or groups to oversee emergency reaction endeavors.

Screen Web-based Entertainment Notices: Utilize web-based entertainment observing apparatuses to follow notices of your image and screen opinion continuously. Early recognition of negative feeling permits you to answer immediately and relieve the effect of a likely emergency.

Answer Speedily and Straightforwardly: In case of an online entertainment emergency, answer expeditiously and straightforwardly to address concerns, give exact data, and console clients. Recognize botches, apologize if essential, and deal arrangements or goals to impacted parties.

Keeping up with Straightforwardness and Credibility

Be Straightforward: Be straightforward and legitimate in your correspondences via virtual entertainment. Reveal any irreconcilable situations, supported content, or associations to keep up with validity and entrust with your crowd.

Connect Truly: Cultivate bona fide cooperations with your crowd by being certified, responsive, and human in your correspondences. Keep away from mechanized reactions or prearranged answers, and endeavor to make significant associations with your adherents.

Share In the background Content: Give your crowd an in the background take a gander at your business to refine your image and fabricate trust. Share stories, photographs, and recordings that exhibit your organization culture, values, and individuals.

Address Negative Input Productively: While getting negative input or analysis via virtual entertainment, answer usefully and expertly. Use criticism as an amazing chance to learn and improve, as opposed to becoming guarded or pompous.

By carrying out web-based entertainment strategies and rules, setting up an emergency reaction plan, and keeping up with straightforwardness and genuineness in your correspondences, you can safeguard your business via online entertainment and construct entrust with your crowd, even in testing circumstances.

Future Trends in Social Media and Business

Arising Stages and Advancements

Expanded Reality (AR) and Computer generated Reality (VR): AR and VR advances are supposed to assume a critical part coming down the line for online entertainment, empowering vivid encounters and intelligent substance. Stages like Snapchat and Instagram have previously presented AR highlights, like channels and focal points, and we can hope to see further combination of AR and VR into online entertainment stages for advertising and commitment purposes.

Live Streaming: Live streaming is turning out to be progressively well known via web-based entertainment stages, permitting organizations to associate with their crowd continuously and feature true, unfiltered content. As innovation improves and transmission capacity builds, we can hope to see more organizations utilizing live gushing for item dispatches, occasions, and in the background content.

Voice and Sound based Stages: With the ascent of brilliant speakers and voice aides, voice and sound based stages are building up some forward momentum in the virtual entertainment space. Stages like Clubhouse, Twitter Spaces, and Facebook Sound Rooms are empowering clients to take part in live sound discussions and conversations. Organizations can use these stages for systems administration, thought initiative, and client commitment.

The Development of Social Business

Social Business Joining: Web-based entertainment stages are progressively coordinating internet business highlights, permitting clients to find, shop, and buy items straightforwardly inside the stage. We can hope to see further progressions in friendly business joining, with stages offering consistent shopping encounters, remembering for application checkout and customized item suggestions.

Shoppable Substance: Brands are utilizing shoppable substance designs, like shoppable posts, stories, and recordings, to drive deals and transformations via web-based entertainment. As friendly business keeps on developing, we can hope to see more creative shoppable substance arrangements and highlights, for example, expanded reality take a stab at encounters and intuitive item inventories.

Powerhouse Promoting and Member Organizations: Powerhouse promoting and member organizations are assuming a key part in driving social business deals. We can hope to see proceeded with development in powerhouse joint efforts and offshoot showcasing programs, with brands utilizing forces to be reckoned with to advance items and drive changes straightforwardly inside virtual entertainment stages.

Expectations for the Future Scene of Online Entertainment

Personalization and Customization: Web-based entertainment stages will keep on focusing on personalization and customization, offering clients custom-made content and encounters in view of their inclinations, inclinations, and ways of behaving. This pattern will stretch out to organizations, with brands utilizing information driven experiences to convey designated content and advertising messages to their crowd.

Security and Information Insurance: With expanding worries around security and information assurance, we can hope to see stricter guidelines and rules administering virtual entertainment stages' utilization of client information. Stages should focus on client protection and straightforwardness in their arrangements and practices to keep up with client trust and consistence with guidelines like GDPR and CCPA.

Broadening of Content Organizations: Web-based entertainment stages will keep on expanding content arrangements to take care of developing client inclinations and ways of behaving. We can hope to see more accentuation on short-structure video content, intelligent encounters, and vaporous substance designs like stories and armadas.

By and large, the eventual fate of virtual entertainment and business will be formed by arising innovations, advancing shopper ways of behaving, and moving administrative scenes. Organizations that stay in front of these patterns and adjust their systems as needs be will be strategically situated to prevail in the dynamic and steadily impacting universe of web-based entertainment.

Conclusion

Synopsis of Central issues:

**Online entertainment offers various advantages for organizations, including expanded brand mindfulness, client commitment, and deals valuable open doors.

**Compelling virtual entertainment methodologies include utilizing stages for brand mindfulness, constructing areas of strength for a presence, and interfacing with interest groups through drawing in happy and connections.

**Organizations ought to screen and examine web-based entertainment measurements to follow execution, distinguish drifts, and refine their techniques in view of information driven bits of knowledge.

**While online entertainment presents open doors for development, organizations should likewise know about possible traps, including negative exposure, managing savages, and lawful and moral contemplations.

**Carrying out web-based entertainment approaches, emergency the board designs, and keeping up with straightforwardness and credibility are fundamental for safeguarding organizations via virtual entertainment and building entrust with crowds.

Last Contemplations on Bridling the Force of Virtual Entertainment for Business Achievement:

In the present computerized age, web-based entertainment has turned into a crucial device for organizations hoping to flourish in a cutthroat scene. By grasping the force of web-based entertainment stages and executing compelling systems, organizations can improve their image presence, draw in with their crowd, and drive significant outcomes.

In any case, accomplishment via virtual entertainment requires something other than posting content — it requires an essential methodology, nonstop checking, and transformation to developing patterns and purchaser inclinations.

By remaining informed about arising advances, embracing social trade open doors, and focusing on personalization and straightforwardness, organizations can situate themselves for long haul outcome in the consistently impacting universe of web-based entertainment.

Eventually, bridling the force of online entertainment for business achievement requires a mix of imagination, examination, and realness. By utilizing these standards and embracing the open doors introduced by virtual entertainment, organizations can open new roads for development, cultivate significant associations with their crowd, and accomplish their objectives in the advanced age.

www.ingramcontent.com/pod-product-compliance
Lightning Source LLC
Chambersburg PA
CBHW050241230526
45470CB00005B/2059